CONTENTS

	Page	(vocal / backing)
CAST LIST	3	-
PERCUSSION NOTES	3	-
SCRIPT and SONG LYRICS	4	-
FULL NARRATION (with songs)	-	1
SONGS (incl. percussion)		
The Bear Song	10	2 8
Just Right	12	3-5 9-11
Someone's Been Eating My Porridge!	14	6 12
Goldilocks Woke Up	17	7 13
COPYRIGHT INFORMATION	20	-

EXTRA RESOURCES

We have provided a number of extra resources to accompany this 'Song and Story' book/CD. **Visit our website at www.outoftheark.co.uk/resources to download**:

- Story/script in a child-friendly font so children can read as they listen to the narrated story *(CD track 1)*
- Mini-books with simplified story (for easy reading) and space to illustrate the story
- Lyric sheets

© 2009 Out of the Ark Ltd

Cast List

Speaking parts:

Narrator   Suitable for a teacher or easily divided into shorter sections for a number of different children.

Goldilocks   Scope for quite a bit of acting. Fair hair would be a bonus.

Mother   One simple line to say.

Daddy Bear   With a deep, gruff voice.

Mummy Bear   Good at making porridge *(only joking!)*

Baby Bear   Small and squeaky. Someone who can act 'shocked' is perfect.

Ideas for non-speaking parts:

There are relatively few speaking parts in this musical, however there are lots of opportunities to involve more children throughout the play. The main body of your performers can stand in the 'choir', with some playing percussion *(see below)*. They should also join in the unison lines of script. You could allocate others to set the scene, dressing as trees to make up the forest.

Percussion Notes

Percussion parts are included for all the music *(see music score)*. Encouraging the children to play along with the songs will enrich their musical experience, helping with co-ordination and teamwork. Within the script are suggested areas where percussion can be used for sound effects – have fun including as many as you like, and encourage the children to compose some of their own. You can also experiment with making other 'instruments' from everyday objects you might find at home or in the classroom.

Script and Song Lyrics

NARRATOR   Once upon a time there was a little girl whose hair was so long and golden that everyone called her 'Goldilocks'.

Every day when Goldilocks went out to play, her mother reminded her not to go near the forest.

MOTHER   Don't go near the forest, you might get lost.

NARRATOR   Deep in the forest was a cottage and in the cottage lived three bears. There was Daddy Bear. He spoke in a great big, deep voice.

DADDY BEAR   I'm great big Daddy Bear!

NARRATOR   There was Mummy Bear. She spoke in a middle-sized voice.

MUMMY BEAR   I'm middle-sized Mummy Bear.

NARRATOR   And there was Baby Bear. He spoke in a squeaky, tiny voice.

BABY BEAR   I'm tiny little Baby Bear.

Song 1.   THE BEAR SONG   CD track 2/8

1 He's a great big daddy bear,
   With great big paws and fuzzy hair,
   He sits upon an enormous chair,
   He's a great big fuzzy daddy bear.

2 She's a middle-sized mummy bear,
   With middle-sized paws and fuzzy hair,
   She sits upon a middle-sized chair,
   She's a middle-sized fuzzy mummy bear.

3 He's a little baby bear,
   With little paws and fuzzy hair,
   He sits upon a little chair,
   He's a little fuzzy baby bear.

© 2009 Out of the Ark Ltd, Surrey KT12 4RQ
CCLI Song No. 5304222

NARRATOR	One morning, Mummy Bear made some porridge, but it was too hot to eat. So the three bears went out for a walk in the forest while it cooled down.
	Meanwhile, Goldilocks had forgotten what her mother had told her and she decided to wander into the forest.[1] She walked and walked until finally she came across the three bears' little cottage.
	Goldilocks looked at the cottage and wondered who might live there. She knocked on the door but there was no answer. She could smell something nice inside, so she climbed in through a window to see what it was.
	On the table were three bowls of porridge.
ALL	A great big bowl, a medium-sized bowl and a tiny little bowl.
NARRATOR	Goldilocks tasted the porridge in the big bowl but she couldn't eat it.
GOLDILOCKS	It's too hot!
NARRATOR	Then she tasted the porridge in the medium-sized bowl but she couldn't eat that either.
GOLDILOCKS	It's too cold!
NARRATOR	Then she tasted the porridge in the little bowl.
GOLDILOCKS	Ahh, this porridge is just right!
NARRATOR	So she ate it all up.

Song 2a. JUST RIGHT (Porridge)   CD track 3/9

Just right, just right, just right for me,
Just right, just right, just right for me.
This porridge is as perfect as porridge could be,
Just right for me!

© 2009 Out of the Ark Ltd, Surrey KT12 4RQ
CCLI Song No. 5304253

---

[1] **Added percussion:** Use cabasas and rustling tissue paper for the leaves on the trees. You could also add some soft whistling for birdsong.

NARRATOR	Goldilocks noticed three chairs by the fireside.
ALL	A great big chair, a medium-sized chair and a tiny little chair.
NARRATOR	She tried to sit on the great big chair but it was too high. Then she sat on the medium-sized chair but that was too high as well.
	When she sat on the little chair, she found that it was just the right height for her.

Song 2b. JUST RIGHT (Chair)   CD track 4/10

Just right, just right, just right for me,
Just right, just right, just right for me.
This chair is as perfect as a chair could be,
Just right for me!

© 2009 Out of the Ark Ltd, Surrey KT12 4RQ
CCLI Song No. 5304253

NARRATOR	But as she wriggled about on the chair, there was a loud crack and the little chair broke into pieces.[2]
	Goldilocks felt very tired. She tip-toed up the windy staircase into the bears' bedroom. Inside the bedroom there were three beds.
ALL	A great big bed, a medium-sized bed and a tiny little bed.
NARRATOR	She climbed onto the great big bed, but she didn't like it.
GOLDILOCKS	It's too hard!
NARRATOR	Then she climbed onto the middle-sized bed, but she didn't like that either.
GOLDILOCKS	It's too soft and squidgy!
NARRATOR	Then she climbed onto the tiny little bed.
GOLDILOCKS	Ahh, this bed is just right for me.

---

[2] **Added percussion:** Use a woodblock or slapstick for the sound of the breaking chair.

Song 2c. JUST RIGHT (Bed) CD track 5/11

Just right, just right, just right for me,
Just right, just right, just right for me.
This bed is as perfect as a bed could be,
Just right for me!

© 2009 Out of the Ark Ltd, Surrey KT12 4RQ
CCLI Song No. 5304253

NARRATOR Goldilocks snuggled down under the covers and it was so warm and cosy that she fell fast asleep.

But as she was sleeping, the three bears arrived home. They went into the kitchen and looked at the bowls on the table. Daddy Bear growled angrily.

DADDY BEAR Someone's been eating my porridge!

MUMMY BEAR Someone's been eating my porridge too!

BABY BEAR Someone's been eating my porridge and they've eaten it all up!

NARRATOR Mummy Bear looked very worried and Baby Bear was very fed up because he was hungry.

NARRATOR Then Daddy Bear noticed his chair.

DADDY BEAR Someone's been sitting in my chair!

MUMMY BEAR Someone's been sitting in my chair too!

BABY BEAR Someone's been sitting in my chair and they've broken it!

NARRATOR Baby Bear was very upset and he started to cry.

The three bears went upstairs to the bedroom. Daddy Bear looked at his bed.

DADDY BEAR Someone's been sleeping in my bed!

MUMMY BEAR Someone's been sleeping in my bed too!

BABY BEAR Someone's been sleeping in my bed and they're still there!!

Song 3.   SOMEONE'S BEEN EATING MY PORRIDGE!

CD track 6/12

1. Someone's been eating my porridge!
   Someone's been eating mine too!
   Someone's been eating mine and it's all gone!
   Oh, what are we to do? Oh, what are we to do?

2. Someone's been sitting in my chair!
   Someone's been sitting in mine too!
   Someone's sat in mine and they've broken it up!
   Oh, what are we to do? Oh, what are we to do?

3. Someone's been sleeping in my bed!
   Someone's been sleeping in mine too!
   Someone's slept in my bed and here they are!
   HERE THEY ARE!
   Oh, what are we to do? Oh, what are we to do?

© 2009 Out of the Ark Ltd, Surrey KT12 4RQ
CCLI Song No. 5304260

NARRATOR Just at that moment, Goldilocks woke up and saw the three bears staring at her. They looked very surprised and Goldilocks was very frightened. She leapt out of bed and ran down the stairs as fast as she could.[3] She ran and ran all the way home, and she never went alone into the forest again.

Song 4.   GOLDILOCKS WOKE UP

CD track 7/13

1. Goldilocks woke up, woke up
   And she couldn't believe her eyes.
   Goldilocks woke up, woke up
   And she got a big surprise.
   She saw three bears, three bears, three brown bears,
   Three bears, three bears, three brown bears!

2. Goldilocks leapt out of bed,
   She was feeling very scared.
   Goldilocks leapt out of bed
   And she rushed off down the stairs
   From those three bears, three bears, three brown bears,
   Three bears, three bears, three brown bears!

---

3   **Added percussion:** Slide beater down glockenspiel as Goldilocks runs downstairs.

3. Goldilocks ran quickly home
   As fast as her legs could run.
   She promised she'd not go out alone
   When she wanted to have some fun.
   Now we've reached the end, our story's done,
   We've reached the end, our story's done!

© 2009 Out of the Ark Ltd, Surrey KT12 4RQ
CCLI Song No. 5304277

The Bear Song

Words and Music by
Niki Davies

With a slice of cool! ♩ = 132 (♪♪ = ♪♩ triplet)

finger clicks

low drum

1. He's a great big dad-dy bear,— with great big paws and fuz-zy hair,— he sits up-on an e-
2. She's a mid-dle-sized mum-my bear,— with mid-dle-sized paws and fuz-zy hair,— she sits up-on a
3. He's a lit-tle ba-by bear,— with lit-tle paws and fuz-zy hair,— he sits up-on a

© 2009 Out of the Ark Ltd, Surrey KT12 4RQ
CCLI Song No. 5304222

-nor - mous chair,_ he's a great big fuz - zy dad - dy bear._
mid - dle - sized chair,_ she's a mid - dle - sized fuz - zy mum - my bear._
lit - tle chair,_ he's a lit - tle fuz - zy ba - by bear._

Just Right

Words and Music by
Niki Davies

Brightly ♩ = 94

Just right, just right, just right for me,

just right, just right, just right for me.

{ 1. This
  2. This
  3. This

© 2009 Out of the Ark Ltd, Surrey KT12 4RQ
CCLI Song No. 5304253

porridge is as perfect as porridge could
chair is as perfect as a chair could
bed is as perfect as a bed could
be, just right for
be,
be,
me!

Someone's Been Eating My Porridge!

Words and Music by
Niki Davies

Steadily ♩ = 190

1° tambourine, 2° castanets, 3° small drum

1. Some-one's been eat-ing my por - - ridge!
2. Some-one's been sit-ting in my chair!
3. Some-one's been sleep-ing in my bed!

Some-one's been eat-ing mine too!
Some-one's been sit-ting in mine too!
Some-one's been sleep-ing in mine too!

© 2009 Out of the Ark Ltd, Surrey KT12 4RQ
CCLI Song No. 5304260

Some-one's been eat-ing mine and it's all gone!
Some-one's sat in mine and they've bro-ken it up!
Some-one's slept in my bed and here they are!

cymbal

Oh, what are we to do? Oh, what are

1.
we to do?

2.
do?

D.%. al Coda

CODA

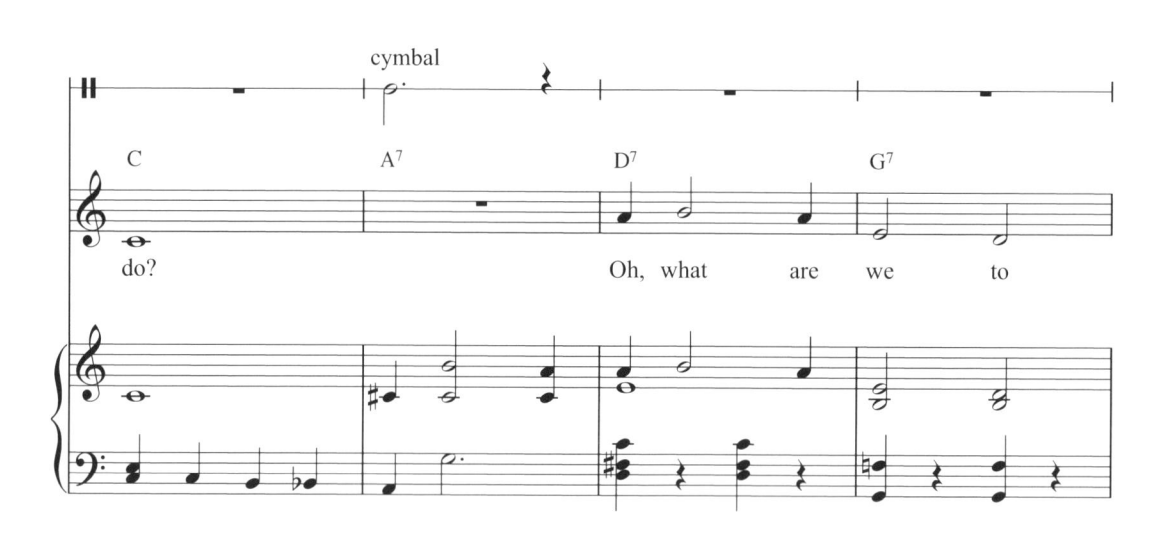

HERE THEY ARE! Oh, what are we to

do? Oh, what are we to

do?

Goldilocks Woke Up

Words and Music by
Niki Davies

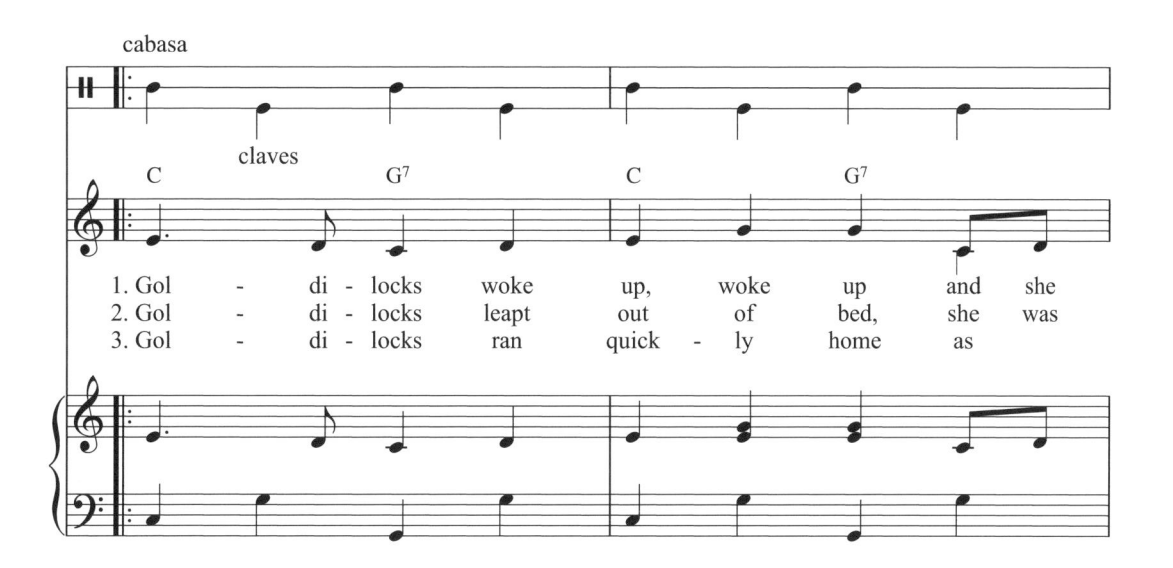

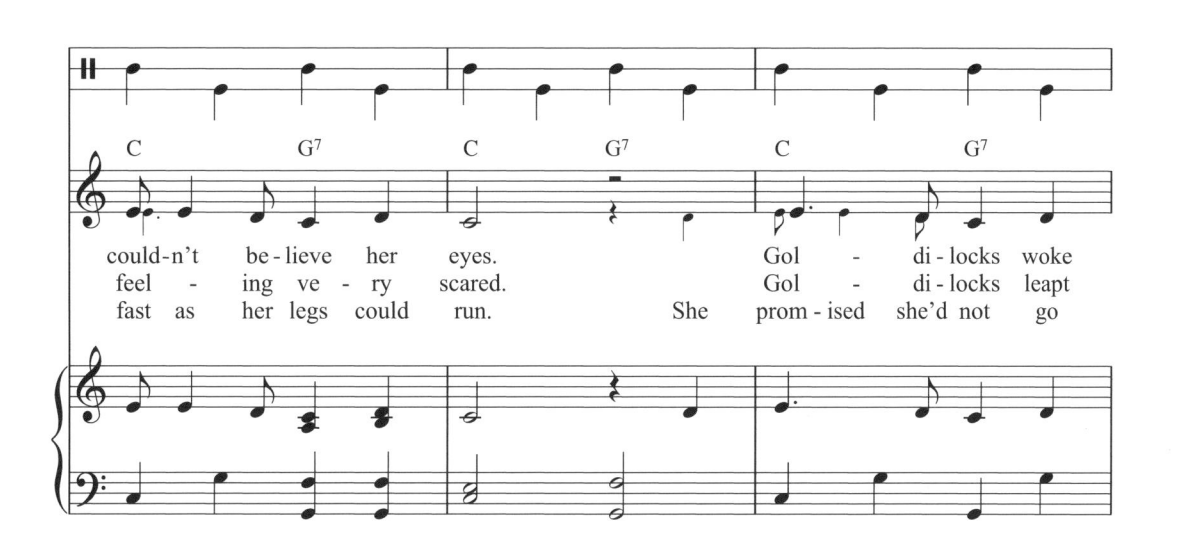

♩ = 170

1. Gol - di - locks woke up, woke up and she could-n't be-lieve her eyes. Gol - di - locks woke
2. Gol - di - locks leapt out of bed, she was feel - ing ve - ry scared. Gol - di - locks leapt
3. Gol - di - locks ran quick - ly home as fast as her legs could run. She prom - ised she'd not go

© 2009 Out of the Ark Ltd, Surrey KT12 4RQ
CCLI Song No. 5304277

up, woke up and she got a big sur-
out of bed and she rushed off down the
out a-lone when she want-ed to have some

triangle

-prise. She saw three bears, three bears,
stairs from those three bears, three bears,
fun. Now we've reached the end, our

three brown bears, three bears,
three brown bears, three bears,
sto-ry's done, we've reached the

| C | A⁷ | Dm⁷ | G⁷ | C |

three bears, three brown bears!
three bears, three brown bears!
end, our sto - ry's done!

1. 2.

| C | G⁷ | C | G⁷ | C | G⁷ | C | G⁷ |

3.

| C | G⁷ | C | G⁷ | C | G⁷ | C |

Copyright & Licensing

VERY IMPORTANT

You are free to use the material in our musicals for all teaching purposes. However the performance of musicals or songs to an audience and the reproduction of scripts, lyrics and music scores are subject to licensing requirements by law. A free licence for certain performances is available on the CD provided with this songbook – see below for details.

Helpful information about licensing can also be found on the following website:

'A Guide to Licensing Copyright in Schools' www.licensing-copyright.org

And remember, we're happy to help. For advice contact our customer services team:

UK: 01932 232 250 International: +44 1932 232 250 copyright@outoftheark.com

(1) Performance of Musicals

The performance of a work involving drama, movement, narrative or dialogue such as a musical requires a specific licence from the publisher. **Your PRS licence does not cover musicals.**

If your school is performing *'Goldilocks and the Three Bears'* by Niki Davies as a musical on school premises, to an audience of staff, pupils and their families, then to simplify the process we have already issued an inclusive licence that grants permission to stage a performance.

If you are performing *'Goldilocks and the Three Bears'* for any other type of audience please contact Out of the Ark Music directly to apply for a performance licence.

(2) Licensing of Audio and Video Recordings

To make an audio or video recording please contact Out of the Ark Music directly.

(3) Other use of the published material

If you are not staging a musical but still intend to use material from the publication then different licences are required:

(a) Reproduction of Song Lyrics or Musical Scores
The following licences from Christian Copyright Licensing Ltd (www.ccli.com) permit photocopying or reproduction of song lyrics and music scores, for example to create song-sheets, overhead transparencies or to use any electronic display medium.

For UK schools: 'Collective Worship Copyright Licence' and 'Music Reproduction Licence.'
For churches: 'Church Copyright and Music Reproduction Licence.'

Please ensure that you log the songs that are used on your copy report. (Organisations that do not hold one of the above licences should contact Out of the Ark Music directly for permission.)

(b) Performance of Songs
If you are not staging a musical but are performing any of our songs for the public on school premises (i.e. for anybody other than staff and pupils) then royalty payments become due. Most schools have an arrangement with the Performing Rights Society (PRS) through their local authority. Organisations that do not have such an arrangement should contact Out of the Ark Music directly.